Between Tads and Toads

Published in 2020 by
The Independent Publishing Network

Illustrations: Yornelys Zambrano
Cover design/layout: Luis Porem

ISBN: 9798551504917
christinemay.com

Between Tads and Toads

Christine May

Prologue

In a distant part of Sussex
there was once a special place
that had not met the real world's face,
where life was incomplex.

In a place off all the roads
there were the Hills and the Pond.
In some houses unparagoned
lived the tads, the frogs and the toads.

The Pondlings

Parading with their parasols
with bluebells in their buttonholes
along the pondside promenade,
life was an endless masquerade!

As kings and queens they pranced around
the charming old-time village ground.
'Isn't this all rather jolly!'
they said as others cried 'Oh Golly!'

But serious business for frogs this was
though others did think them at quite a loss.
What they were doing the frogs knew well
and wearing it right, they did look swell!

Treating facts as trivial
and trivia as literal,
they always knew how to seem smart
and look like wandering works of Art.

With ballet classes every morn'
to up their jumps and trim their form,
for if they did do really well
there was the local swish hotel.

There they with luck could gain a place,
if they moved round with perfect grace.
With arabesques and black bow tie,
they hoped to catch each pondling's eye.

There was one frog in particular,
the most unique object d'art.
Pretty Frederic was the one
who did stand out from everyone.

He dressed with class and perfect match
and wore it just a bit detached.
Precisely proportioned, unlike other frogs,
he could wear any rags, still gorgeous he was.

His skin was of that palest green,
that anyone had ever seen.
With that unique tint of mint
he would make anyone's heart sprint.

With eyes as frogs' are wont to be,
but his were the saddest you'd ever see.
Not like the other frogs' by the pond,
to his eyes no one seemed to respond.

When traipsing down the town's high street
he wore his favourite brogues so neat,
looking like the fairest of days,
but telling himself he's too fat, as always.

Shopping trousers, shirts and socks
and some new fragrance to top it off.
There in town there was no strife,
for when he shopped, he shopped for life.

But Friday it was and this meant ice-creams,
with not much thought on careers or such themes
So much nicer and easy to do,
ice-creams frogs ate with no attempt to rue.

For frogs and jobs did not go well,
toil and toads did better gel.
So the frogs swanned off, minding not so much
the other pondlings, or darlings, or the such.

In their opinion, the tads were petite
and the toads quite ravishing beings to meet.
Nothing was quite like being admired
by other pondlings finely attired.

And the toads were marvellously dressed,
thus they stood out from the rest.
They did like tailored tweed suits very much,
to go with a Jermyn Street shirt, for a touch!

The toads were picky, indeed one could say
they had their firm tastes to always obey.
In those institutions they serve and belong,
there, tweed could never go wrong.

Picnic Time

The frogs and toads did frequently meet,
especially on days when the frogs felt upbeat
and this particular, sunny fine day
they felt like a picnic 'Away, hooray!'

So after consulting a trustworthy toad,
plans for a picnic were soon to be sowed.
Excited small tads jumped right up and down
and soon all were set to leave the dear town.

As afternoon came, their motors in tow,
towards the Hills they opted to go
and after a pleasant, short little trot
they soon set up a beautiful spot.

The toads had brought a basket of scones
and rolls and hams and some croutons.
Nothing had they forgotten to bring
for a picnic was a serious thing!

The tads, who were the very young
with just-developed leg and lung,
were eager to try out their limbs
at something different than their swims.

Leapfrog was their foremost choice,
in hopscotch then they did rejoice.
So much spree, so much joy
they did in these two games employ.

Hopping on one leg was fun,
but soon they all had one game won.
The tads sat down, well-exercised,
but soon a new game was devised.

'Roll down the Hills, the fastest wins!'
and as the romp again begins,
the toads amuse themselves with Pimm's.
Battenburg rolls were their sweet whims.

And Frederic had the sweetest tooth
of all the frogs, it's quite the truth,
but hidden in his figure slim
a sadness lurked in his within.

Following the sweet, sweet cake
he would completely spurn and hate
himself as well as all the rest,
that painful feeling in his chest.

He'd have to swim a hundred laps
across the pond, there's no perhaps,
for Frederic could just not sustain
the thought of fat on his small frame.

He tried to be like other frogs.
Play games, not go for any jogs,
but nothing fun did make him sane.
Not even one short croquet game.

For games and fun were not for Fred.
He never felt high-spirited,
but no one saw Fred's secret fight
and thought that everything seemed right.

Such was that yearly picnic time
with toads and tads and frogs in rhyme,
and in the eve you might just find
a slumped down toad with pipe unwind.

The Swimming Race

The annual summer swimming race
on every June the eight took place.
So long awaited by the frogs,
they'd purchased some new bathing togs.

Oh, how they dared to thus appear,
showing off in their new gear,
stretching, toning, flexing thighs
in front of all the pondlings' eyes.

When on the shore the frogs turned hunks,
the toads would swap their suits to trunks
and tads would get to show them all
their latest strokes and all their crawl.

They'd practised all their tiny lives,
especially their deep-pond dives,
and if they didn't win first prize
they'd be all tears and endless cries.

So all are set to start the race;
ten tads, ten frogs, ten toads in place.
All the pondlings stand on land,
cheering, chanting feet in sand.

Excitement's in the summer air.
A pistol fires, the fanfare!
In three lanes, amphibs divide.
Up to test, their swim and glide!

The tads all swim the speed of flight
and cross the pond with all their might.
They swim the length all back again
before the toads reached half-way lane.

The frogs were slightly more perturbed
by how they were by all observed.
It came as no real great surprise
that they would win the second prize.

The toads came last, but everyone knows
toads and sports are really foes.
They'd left their tadhoods long behind
and were for gentler times inclined.

Such was that day of the big race
with tads and frogs and toads in chase.
To trace it back to the begin'
you see how things had always been.

No real dangers, no strange sounds.
Nothing changes, no one drowns.
Thus they lived their fair old lives,
apart from one with different drives.

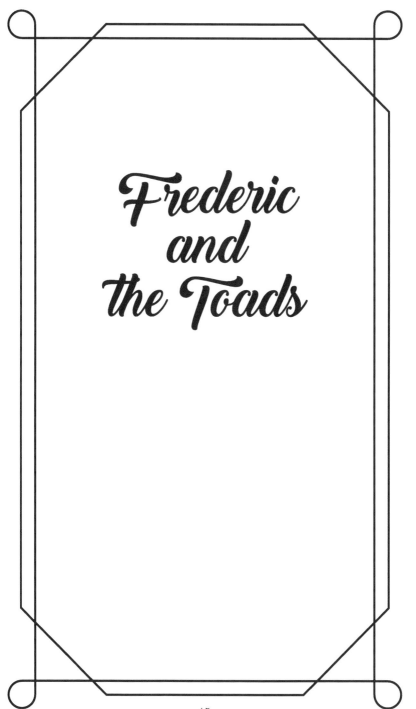

Frederic and the Toads

Thursday nights Fred visited *Club Delights*
for some distractions from his plights.
There, a bar-frog with no strife
for when he danced, he danced for life.

The toads would always turn his way
for he looked like a summer's day.
For Fred had the beautiful eyes and the guise
and toads could never see through such lies.

This night it was a busy night.
Some business toads, so socialite,
with briefcases of high-priced leather
had found there way somehow down nether.

This was one very rare address
where toads and frogs would share interest.
It was just so remarkable,
their contrast was considerable.

For frogs only had one special desire;
to look so charming, they never did tire.
So far from the toads with well-earnt degrees,
frogs did not seek academic expertise.

They felt they knew all there was to know
and instead tried to put on a beautiful show.
While toads enjoyed facts to freely impart,
the frogs spent their time being pieces of Art.

For a ravishing look was all that it took
for a toad to get firmly caught on their hook.
To have read every book, frogs needn't prove,
the toads anyway would always approve.

There was a pull in a toad's demeanour,
their stoutness and clout and their odour
and toads in their turn would always adore
these wandering fine petits fours.

A particular dashing, black-briefcased toad,
really quite clever and so à la mode,
approached pretty Frederic with this elegance:
'Would you, darling, perchance care to dance?'

Really the toads no intent had to smarm.
It had just become part of their daily charm,
but Fred liked this style, so in this request
he without doubt of a blink acquiesced.

For Fred did feel bored and he liked a fling
and dancing was such a virtuous thing
and since both the species together consented
this certain connection was doubly contented.

But in Fred's small heart he invariably knew,
he was one of those exceptional few
who simply in clubs did just not belong –
there was nothing that could be more wrong.

He did feel too good for all of that stuff,
but nothing was never just quite enough.
And flings took up time and were fun and so
they kept him in track and always on go.

He joined them for dinners and fruity wine,
but left the puddings and gateaux divine.
He didn't quite know why he joined at all,
but sometimes he felt the need to enthral.

That is the story of Fred and the toads.
with many hellos in fashionable modes
No one still knows what inside him on-goes,
but the sadness in eye always forebodes.

Wintertime

When winter came upon the pond
and snow had fallen far beyond
and brought about an icy floor,
the skates came out, before the thaw.

Flying past the pondlings by,
a pirouette into the sky;
the ballet had helped the frogs acquire
the graciousness they deemed so high.

But Fred was struggling in his tights.
This time too high he aimed his sights.
Though he was usually quite precise,
he did fall straight onto the ice.

And badly hurt his knee in the fall.
But appearance was first and much above all,
he skated off fast, threw scarf over shoulder,
wishing that no one had seen his trip over.

After all the skating was done
the day had really just begun,
so a trip towards the Hills was planned
for winter games of every brand.

The tads would bring their wooden sleigh
and frogs their skis, this wintry day.
The toads, however, did not bring
a single extra sporty thing.

For toads and sports did not go well.
They thought it was an utter hell
to exercise their podgy limbs.
They did prefer their goodly gins.

The frogs for this new year had bought
new ski-suits for the ski-resort.
In this gear they were the craze
attracting every creature's gaze.

They flew like athletes down the hill
skiing one by one with skill,
while the tads would fit as many they could
onto their sleigh of beech-tree wood.

Tumbling down, all racketing,
forgetting simply everything.
They lost their track and path in sight
and dropped a tad, oh what a fright!

But in the end they all were fine
and joined the toads for their mulled wine.
For tads the taste was odd and old,
they did not drink as they were told.

The frogs had brought their flasks of tea,
for healthy was their one decree
and to Christmas wine they'd not submit.
It was more important to stay fit.

But all with something to drink in hand,
they toasted their happy health, so grand,
and Frederic joined their cluster of clink
though he felt like on the uttermost brink.

After all the drinking was done,
return to home to warm up some,
for legs and limbs had got quite cold,
especially for the passive toad.

So bubble baths for tads and frogs.
For toads a rest by burning logs.
Thus they ended those fair days
of happy, snowy escapades!

But all was not as well as it seemed
for next day Fred's inside just screamed.
He took a walk to clear his mind,
but deep in woods the weather was unkind.

The freezing air cut through his skin,
and blew straight to his soul within.
He came into an open spot
where all the snow'd been left, unspoilt.

And towering around were tall pine trees
with fallen branches, dressed by the freeze.
He took a branch and began to write
some letters in the floor of white.

F..R..E..D..E..R..I..C.

For everyone to clearly see,

and he lay down, curved up in 'C'

and that night sensed eternity.

The Rescue

'Wake up, wake up, my little friend
or I shall cry 'till my life's end,'
a little female screamed and shout'
and shook Fred's shoulders in and out.

And Fred, though frozen stiff all over,
with one eye saw her arched 'cross over,
and she was such a pretty sight,
although a frog, she looked a sprite.

So Frederic tried his eye ajar,
but looked quite dead, gazing afar.
'Oh, show me that you are alive!'
She set about him to revive.

She blew into his mouth so blue,
and Frederic came to life anew.
And when his gasp of breath she heard,
she stopped, was almost lost for word.

She took her wool coat off for Fred
and lift' him up, support' his head.
'God! You look so lifeless, white!'
She wrapped him in her coat so tight.

'I'm sorry I can't carry you,
I'm far too small to so pursue,
a wheelbarrow I will go get
and be back faster than a jet!'

She ran for home, she ran and ran
and prayed and hoped as tears began
and Frederic lay there wrapped in coat.
'tween life and death he did still float.

Panting she returned at speed,
and tipped Fred in, so to proceed.
She ran and pushed him just as much
to make them move through snow and slush.

Her house was just a short way off,
through woods and past a great big trough.
She came into her snow-clad path,
and thought she'd make a steaming bath.

When through the doors she dragged him in,
the homely warmth soon made his skin
return to just a greener tone
than when she'd found him lifeless, lone.

Soon Frederic opened both his eyes
quite slowly and with such surprise,
he found himself inside a home
that felt and smelt like heaven's dome.

How cosy on a rug he lay
by fire and with tea on tray.
With oil of lavender and of rose,
she rubbed his feet and all his toes.

'Say not a word, don't even squeak.
You are a frog, still very weak.
Just lie down here and let me tend
and may I soon become a friend.'

Fred lay there still and deeply dreamed
how like this place to heaven seemed.
Was he alive or had he gone
to where all go when called upon?

Frederic Speaks

When light arrived again she spoke
and on his head gave him a stroke.
'You've slept so long it has become
a full new day, my little chum.

Please tell me why you went to sleep
in darkest woods, in snow so deep?'
To this, Frederic found it hard
to find reply, still on his guard.

How could he form into some speech
things so far inside to reach,
but try he might as well today
for what's to gain or lose this way?

'Oh, little angel frog, so sweet
I trust that you keep things discreet,
I simply could not bear to be
where there's nought of joy for me.

I do feel empty, sad inside
There's nothing to astrive,' he cried.
'There is no point when in the end
we all just leave this life, ascend.

I look like this, am clever too,
but it's as if nobody knew.
For no one seems to see that I
am special and aspire so high.

There's no one here to understand
and no one here to hold my hand,
no one I can call my friend.
I can't continue to pretend.'

At this lament, Fred shed tears
as he let go of all his fears,
but to this listening, frog-like saint
he emptied himself without restraint.

What had he ever so freely said?
Would the frog girl turn to hate him instead?
He waited, eager, for her reply
and it came with a long and emphatic sigh.

'Maybe no one has said that you are
in sight appearing like a star,
but my dear frog that's not enough
to bring you joy, it's such a bluff.

To be an empty, pretty shell
without a beating heart is hell.
When every thought's on how you appear
and not how you feel or if you're sincere.

It's hard to feel awake, alive
when you deny your inmost drive
and think that just a pretty face
will find yourself a hearty place.

You have to find your joy elsewhere
in words or art or friends or prayer,
not in just a face that wanes,
but something for the heart or brains.'

Fred had listened with his big eyes
and felt that what she said was wise,
but how to change a life that's built
on something fleeting that shall wilt?

Overcome by a weight profound
he had to change his values round.
He had to make life more worthwhile;
to somehow strive for heart, not style.

The End

Acknowledgement

This book would not exist without the unwavering conviction and support of Luis Porem. From championing the publication of this book in the first place, he has been with me every step of the way. His dedicated hard work and aesthetic sensibility was especially invaluable when working with developing the illustrations for this book, and for working on the cover and layout.

Thank you for believing in Frederic's universal struggle. You have my eternal gratitude.

Christine May is an Anglo-Swedish writer, poet and copywriter. No matter what style, she seeks to dig deep in her writing to let the unknown become visible and the truth become known.

christinemay.com